DISCARDED

6-98	DATE DUE		
JUN 1 8	OCT 17		
JUL 13	NOV 28		
AUG 1 1	MAY 5		
OCT 1 2	FEB 7		
	FEB 27		
NOV 16	NOV 8		
NOV 27			
DEC 3 0			
MAR 1 2			
MAY 1 1			
JUN 0 7			
JUL 23			
AUG 2 0			
SEP 0 6			
NOV 25			
JUL 3 1			
AUG 16			

Little Book of Questions & Answers

Animals

Manufactured in U.S.A.

8 7 6 5 4 3 2 1

ISBN: 1-56173-470-5

Contributing Writer: Teri Crawford Jones

Illustrations: T. F. Marsh

HTS BOOKS
AN IMPRINT OF FOREST HOUSE™
School & Library Edition

Can parrots really talk?

Parrots talk to each other in squawks. When a parrot speaks like you, it just copies your voice. It does not know what it is saying. A parrot is a good *mimic*.

Does an elephant drink through its trunk?

An elephant's trunk is its nose, not a built-in drinking straw. Elephants suck water into their trunks and squirt it into their mouths.

What does a monkey do with its tail?

A monkey uses its long tail to keep its balance when it swings through the trees. At night, monkeys wrap their tails around tree branches so they don't fall when they are asleep.

Why do tigers have stripes?

Tigers live and hunt among the trees and tall grasses of the jungle. The stripes on the tiger help it blend with the striped shadows of the leaves and grasses as sunlight shines through the jungle.

How do giraffes eat and drink?

The giraffe's long neck and legs help it reach the tender leaves of tall trees. To take a drink of water from a river or spring, a giraffe must spread its front legs apart and bend its head way, way down.

Why do chimpanzees like to eat bananas?

Chimps love fruit. A banana is an especially sweet fruit treat for a chimp. Bananas grow in the jungle where wild chimps live. A chimp has hands that are almost like ours, so it is able to peel a banana.

Why do chickens peck?

Chickens eat seeds and grains. They do not see very well, so they will peck at anything that looks like food. Chickens often swallow small pebbles, which do not harm them at all!

Why are pigs so noisy?

Pigs oink for food. They grunt softly when they eat. They squeal loudly when they are excited or frightened. Oinking, grunting, and squealing are some of the ways that pigs "talk" to each other.

Why are cows always chewing?

When a cow swallows a mouthful of grass, the grass goes into the cow's stomach and later comes back up into the cow's mouth for more chewing. Then the cow swallows the grass again.

Why do ducks waddle?

A duck has short legs, flat paddle-feet, and a wide body. Its legs are sort of far apart, too. When a duck walks, it sways from side to side. It can't help it. Ducks are made for swimming, not walking!

Do turtles live in water all the time?

Turtles live both on land and in water. They breathe like land animals, but they can stay under water for a long time. Turtles eat foods that are found in or near ponds, so they stay close to ponds.

What does a baby frog look like?

Frogs begin life as tadpoles. At first they are just a head with a tail. But as they get older, they grow legs and their tail disappears. Then one day, they are frogs from head to toe!

Is a zebra just a striped horse?

The zebra is not a horse, but it *does* belong to the same family as the horse. Besides having stripes, a zebra's mane is short and bristly. A horse has a long, shaggy mane. Their tails are different, too.

Why do antelopes live in herds?

A hungry lion would find it easy to sneak up on one antelope. In a herd, some can be "guards" while others are resting or eating. When the guards sense danger, they give a sign. The antelopes all run!

How big is an ostrich egg?

The egg of the ostrich is the biggest egg in the world. It may weigh as much as three and one half pounds. It is about the size of a cantaloupe!

Why do squirrels get into bird feeders?

Squirrels love to eat the seeds that we set out for birds. A squirrel does not know that the bird feeder is meant for birds only; it just knows that it is a great place to find lots of food.

Why do puppies sniff everything?

Dogs use their sense of smell to learn about the world around them. Because the world is new to a young puppy, the puppy needs to smell everything and everyone it meets.

How does a robin find a worm?

When a robin cocks its head, it seems to listen for food, but it is really *looking* for food. A robin's eyes are on the sides of its head. It must tilt its head to the side to look at the ground.

What do ants do inside an anthill?

The hill of an anthill is not the main part of the ants' home. Under it is an ant city that is made of tiny tunnels and rooms. Food is stored in some rooms; ant eggs and babies are kept in other rooms.

Why do rabbits seem so twitchy and nervous?

A rabbit's nose, whiskers, and big ears pick up sounds and smells. Twitching ears and a trembling nose mean that a rabbit is on the lookout for danger. Rabbits are food for lots of bigger animals.

How big is a baby mouse?

Since mice are very small, their babies are very, *very* small! Newborn mice are about the size of a fingernail. A baby mouse is born blind, deaf, and without fur. It is pink all over!

Where do eagles build their nests?

Eagles build their big nests in very tall trees or on the edge of a rocky cliff. The eagle's nest is built of sticks and branches, which the eagle may have broken from trees.

Why do we say a grizzly bear is "grizzly?"

To be "grizzled" is to be sprinkled with flecks of gray. A man's beard that is flecked with gray is a "grizzly" beard. The tips of the hairs in a grizzly bear's dark fur are often grayish white.

Is a wolf pup like a pet puppy?

A wolf pup plays, barks, growls, and tugs on its mother's ears and tail. It tumbles around with its brothers and sisters. You can tell that dogs and wolves belong to the same animal family.

Why do owls come out at night?

Owls have very good hearing and they can see in the dark. Their favorite food is mice, which come out at night to look for food. Owls stay up to hunt for the mice and other small animals.

Where do deer sleep?

Even though deer may not stay in the forest all day, they go to the edge of the forest to sleep. Their best hiding place is in the low brush where they lie down on the soft leaves and grasses.

How many babies does an opossum have?

An opossum may have as many as 18 babies at one time. Young opossums ride around on their mother's back. Her fur and body heat keep them warm.

Why does a lion tamer use a whip and chair?

The cracking sound of the whip tells the lion which tricks to do. If the lion swats its paw—and sharp claws—at the tamer, the tamer can push the paw away with the chair.

How does a seal learn to play a tune?

Seals are smart. With lots of practice they can remember when to honk the horns that will play a short tune. When the seal does a good job, its trainer gives it a treat—usually a piece of fish.

Are tusks the only teeth an elephant has?

An elephant has four teeth inside its mouth, not counting its tusks. Each of these four teeth is 12 inches long and weighs nine pounds! That's about the size of a newborn human baby!

Does a scorpion sting or bite?
A scorpion stings! A sharp point on the end of its tail is its poisonous stinger. Scorpions sting to catch food. They will also sting their enemy if they are in danger.

How did the jackrabbit get its name?
Jackrabbits have very long ears. Their ears look like donkey ears! A boy donkey is called a jack. The jackrabbit's long ears help it hear the slightest noises so it can escape from danger in the desert.

Are vultures good for anything?
Vultures are one of nature's "garbage collectors." They eat animals that have died or that have been killed. Without vultures to clean up, parts of nature would not smell or look very nice!

How do penguins keep their eggs warm?
Some penguins lay their eggs in nests. But the father emperor penguin holds its egg on top of its feet so that it does not touch the ice. A flap of warm belly skin covers the egg and keeps it warm.

Do a polar bear's feet get cold?
A polar bear has fur on the soles of its feet. This fur does two things. It keeps the bear's feet warm and it helps to keep the bear from slipping and sliding on the ice. It is like wearing snow boots!

What happens to the arctic fox in summer?
The arctic fox has white fur during winter to match the snow. Its fur turns brown or gray-blue in summer to match the bare ground. The same thing happens to some other arctic animals.

Can an electric eel shock a person?

Yes, but eels are shy. An eel would probably hide from you if you were scuba diving near it. The shock of an electric eel would not kill a human, but it can light a light bulb!

Do all fish have scales?

No. The shark has a different kind of skin covering that is made of the same thing as the shark's teeth. A shark's skin looks smooth, but it is not. If you rub it the wrong way, you will be badly cut.

What is the biggest fish in the sea?

A shark called the whale shark is the biggest fish in the sea. It may grow to be 45 feet long—or longer. That's longer than a city bus! Whale sharks are gentle. They are not scary like other sharks.

Do my pets dream?

Scientists believe that most animals dream about things in their lives. Dogs may dream about running or eating. Cats may dream about hunting or playing. Your pet may dream about *you!*